# Women in Information Technology

# Major Women in Science

# Women in Information Technology

Shaina Indovino

Mason Crest

Mason Crest
450 Parkway Drive, Suite D
Broomall, Pennsylvania 19008
www.masoncrest.com

Printed and bound in the United States of America.

9 8 7 6 5 4 3 2

Series ISBN: 978-1-4222-2923-1
ISBN: 978-1-4222-2928-6
ebook ISBN: 978-1-4222-8897-9

The Library of Congress has cataloged the
        hardcopy format(s) as follows:

        Library of Congress Cataloging-in-Publication Data

Indovino, Shaina Carmel.
  Women in information technology / Shaina Indovino.
      pages cm. – (Major women in science)

  Audience: Grade 7 to 8.
  Includes bibliographical references and index.
    ISBN 978-1-4222-2928-6 (hardcover) – ISBN 978-1-4222-8897-9 (ebook) – ISBN 978-1-4222-2923-1 (series)
  1. Information technology–Biography–Juvenile literature. 2. Women information scientists–Biography–Juvenile literature. 3. Information technology–Vocational guidance–Juvenile literature. I. Title.
  T58.5.I5126 2014
  004.092'52–dc23
                            2013011153

Produced by Vestal Creative Services.
www.vestalcreative.com

# Contents

# Introduction

Have you wondered about how the natural world works? Are you curious about how science could help sick people get better? Do you want to learn more about our planet and universe? Are you excited to use technology to learn and share ideas? Do you want to build something new?

Scientists, engineers, and doctors are among the many types of people who think deeply about science and nature, who often have new ideas on how to improve life in our world.

We live in a remarkable time in human history. The level of understanding and rate of progress in science and technology have never been greater. Major advances in these areas include the following:

- Computer scientists and engineers are building mobile and Internet technology to help people access and share information at incredible speeds.
- Biologists and chemists are creating medicines that can target and get rid of harmful cancer cells in the body.
- Engineers are guiding robots on Mars to explore the history of water on that planet.
- Physicists are using math and experiments to estimate the age of the universe to be greater than 13 billion years old.
- Scientists and engineers are building hybrid cars that can be better for our environment.

Scientists are interested in discovering and understanding key principles in nature, including biological, chemical, mathematical, and physical aspects of our world. Scientists observe, measure, and experiment in a systematic way in order to test and improve their understanding. Engineers focus on applying scientific knowledge and math to find creative solutions for technical problems and to develop real products for people to use. There are many types of engineering, including computer, electrical, mechanical, civil, chemical, and biomedical engineering. Some people have also found that studying science or engineering can help them succeed in other professions such as law, business, and medicine.

Both women and men can be successful in science and engineering. This book series highlights women leaders who have made significant contributions across many scientific fields, including chemistry, medicine, anthropology, engineering, and physics. Historically, women have faced barriers to training and building careers in science,

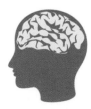

6

which makes some of these stories even more amazing. While not all barriers have been overcome, our society has made tremendous progress in educating and advancing women in science. Today, there are schools, organizations, and resources to enable women to pursue careers as scientists or engineers at the highest levels of achievement and leadership.

The goals of this series are to help you:

1. Learn about women scientists, engineers, doctors, and inventors who have made a major impact in science and our society
2. Understand different types of science and engineering
3. Explore science and math in school and real life

You can do a lot of things to learn more about science, math, and engineering. Explore topics in books or online, take a class at school, go to science camp, or do experiments at home. More important, talk to a real scientist! Call or e-mail your local college to find students and professors. They would love to meet with you. Ask your doctors about their education and training. Or you can check out these helpful resources:

- *Nova* has very cool videos about science, including profiles on real-life women scientists and engineers: www.pbs.org/wgbh/nova.
- *National Geographic* has excellent photos and stories to inspire people to care about the planet: science.nationalgeographic.com/science.
- Here are examples of online courses for students, of which many are free to use:
  1. Massachusetts Institute of Technology (MIT) OpenCourseWare highlights for high school: http://ocw.mit.edu/high-school
  2. Khan Academy tutorials and courses: www.khanacademy.org.
  3. Stanford University Online, featuring video courses and programs for middle and high school students: online.stanford.edu.

Other skills will become important as you get older. Build strong communication skills, such as asking questions and sharing your ideas in class. Ask for advice or help when needed from your teachers, mentors, tutors, or classmates. Be curious and resilient: learn from your successes and mistakes. The best scientists do.

Learning science and math is one of the most important things that you can do in school. Knowledge and experience in these areas will teach you how to think and how the world works and can provide you with many adventures and paths in life. I hope you will explore science—you could make a difference in this world.

*Ann Lee-Karlon, PhD*
*President*
*Association for Women in Science*
*San Francisco, California*

# 1

# What Does It Take to Work in Information Technology?

**H**ave you ever wondered how a computer works? If you look inside, you will see the many different pieces that make up a computer. To someone who doesn't know what each of those pieces does, a computer might seem like a magic box.

The pieces that make up a computer are known as hardware. Any physical item that you can hold in your hand is a piece of hardware. Hardware is needed for a computer to even turn on.

Computer programmers work with software, or information that is stored on the hard pieces inside a computer's case. It is called software because it is not something you can touch or feel. Even though hardware is needed for a computer to turn on, software is needed for it to function. Operating systems are the most complex type of computer program. They allow other computer programs to run. Two examples are Microsoft Windows and Macintosh OS X.

A computer scientist has made every single program you use on your computer. Every website you look at was programmed by someone who worked in information technology. Any time you write a report with a word processor, you have a computer programmer to thank!

A computer doesn't always have to sit on your desk. Some computers are very small. Most electronic systems contain computers. Some examples include an oven, a television, and a car. Even your mobile phone has its own programs. In fact, your mobile phone is actually a tiny computer that can fit into the palm of your hand.

As the world becomes more reliant on technology, we need more computer experts. If you are interested in programming or fixing computers, consider pursuing a job in information technology!

# Why Work in Information Technology?

Information technology (IT)—the name of the **industry** that creates computer hardware and software—is used today in every single scientific field. Many scientists use very high-level math to understand what they are working on, and computers help them to do this.

Computers aren't just used by scientists, though. Pretty much everyone else uses computers, too, from bankers to artists. Just a few decades ago, these

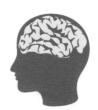

computers would have been impossible to make. But the world of technology is constantly changing.

That's why information technology workers are in high demand, and they are paid very well. Information technology includes many different kinds of jobs, and the field is always expanding.

# Education

The level of education you need depends on which type of information technology you want to enter. Some jobs will only require some college or a bachelor's degree. Others will require a master's or doctorate degree. This chart from the U.S. Bureau of Labor Statistics shows a range of jobs, the education required for each, and how much you can expect to be paid.

# Character

No matter which area of information technology you choose to become a part of, you'll need to possess certain character traits. O-net (www.onetonline.org) lists these traits as being most necessary for working in this field:

- **complex problem-solving:** Identifying complex problems and reviewing related information to develop and evaluate options and put solutions into practice.
- **critical thinking:** Using logic and reasoning to identify the strengths and weaknesses of different solutions, conclusions, or approaches to problems.
- **judgment and decision-making:** Considering the **relative** costs and benefits of possible actions in order to choose the most appropriate one.
- **active listening:** Giving full attention to what other people are saying, taking time to understand the points being made, asking questions as appropriate, and not interrupting at inappropriate times.
- **reading comprehension:** Understanding written sentences and paragraphs in work-related documents.
- **time management:** Managing one's own time and the time of others.

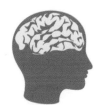

| job | what they do | degree required for entry-level | median pay in 2010 |
|---|---|---|---|
| Computer and Information Research Scientists | Computer and information research scientists invent and design new technology and find new uses for existing technology. They study and solve complex problems in computing for business, science, medicine, and other uses. | doctoral or professional degree | $100,660 |
| Computer Programmers | Computer programmers write code to create software programs. They turn the program designs created by software developers and engineers into instructions that a computer can follow. | bachelor's degree | $71,380 |
| Computer Support Specialists | Computer support specialists provide help and advice to people and organizations using computer software or equipment. Some, called technical support specialists, provide support for employees within their organization. Others, called help-desk technicians, assist non-IT users who are having computer problems. | some college (no degree) or bachelor's degree | $46,260 |

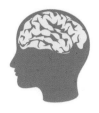

| | | | |
|---|---|---|---|
| Computer Systems Analysts | Computer systems analysts study an organization's current computer systems and procedures and make recommendations to management to help the organization operate more efficiently and effectively. They bring business and information technology (IT) together by understanding the needs and limitations of both. | bachelor's degree | $77,740 |
| Database Administrators | Database administrators use software to store and organize data, such as financial information and customer shipping records. They make sure that data are available to users and are secure from unauthorized access. | bachelor's degree | $73,490 |
| Information Security Analysts, Web Developers, and Computer Network Architects | Information security analysts, web developers, and computer network architects all use information technology (IT) to advance their organization's goals. Security analysts ensure a firm's information stays safe from cyberattacks. Web developers create websites to help firms have a public face. Computer network architects create the internal networks all workers within organizations use. | bachelor's degree | $75,660 |

| | | | |
|---|---|---|---|
| Network and Computer Systems Administrators | Network and computer systems administrators are responsible for the day-to-day operation of an organization's computer networks. They organize, install, and support an organization's computer systems, including local area networks (LANs), wide area networks (WANs), network segments, intranets, and other data communication systems. | bachelor's degree | $69,160 |
| Software Developers | Software developers are the creative minds behind computer programs. Some develop the applications that allow people to do specific tasks on a computer or other device. Others develop the underlying systems that run the devices or control networks. | bachelor's degree | $90,530 |

• **active learning:** Understanding the **implications** of new information for both current and future problem-solving and decision-making.

Do any of these traits sound like you? In the chapters that follow, as you read about some of the women leaders in this field, see if you recognize anything you have in common with them. If so—and you like working with computers—this might be a career for you to consider.

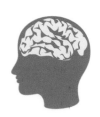

# Words to Know

**Industry:** a particular kind of business activity.
**Relative:** considered in proportion or relation to something else.
**Implications:** likely consequences.

# Find Out More

Sande, Warren, and Carter Sande. *Hello World! Computer Programming for Kids and Other Beginners.* Greenwich, Conn.: Manning, 2009.

Briggs, Jason R. *Python for Kids: A Playful Introduction to Programming.* San Francisco, Calif.: No Starch, 2013.

Education Portal, "How to Become an Information Technology IT Specialist"
www.education-portal.com/articles/How_to_Become_an_Information_Technology_IT_Specialist.html

Technology Colleges, "How to Become an IT Professional"
www.technology-colleges.info/index2.html

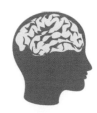

# 2

# Ada Lovelace (Augusta Ada King):

# First Computer Programmer

Today, computers are very small and powerful. In Augusta Ada King's time, however, early computers were not much like they are today. They did not use electronic signals to run. Instead, some of the earliest computers used cards with holes punched out of them. Next came mechanical computers, which used gears and levers. Augusta Ada King (known to her family and friends as Ada) came up with ways to program these earliest computers.

Ada was born on December 10, 1815, in England. Her life was very different from her peers', because her mother and father divorced when she was a little girl, something that was uncommon in the nineteenth century. Ada's family was a prominent and wealthy one, which gave Ada more opportunities than she might have had otherwise. Her father was Lord Byron, the famous poet. Nevertheless, her mother struggled to be respected as a single parent.

Ada was very smart and did well in school. Her mother believed in her daughter's abilities, and she helped Ada get the education she would need to be successful in mathematics, even though at the time, female mathematicians were rare. As Ada grew up, she worked with researchers and scientists, getting the training she needed to be successful.

In 1935, Ada married William King. Because William was a **baron**, Augusta became a baroness. Later, he would become the Earl of Lovelace, and she would become the Countess, a title she held until her death. Because she was a member of the nobility in England, Ada was treated with more respect than she might have been otherwise, which was a major reason for her success. She became as well known in the scientific world.

In 1842, Charles Babbage, a fellow mathematician and scientist, asked Ada to translate a paper about an **analytical** engine—one of the first computers—into English. The engine described in the paper had not yet been built, but the paper explained how it would function. Translating the paper into English was important because it would help Charles Babbage gain the funding he needed to build the engine.

When Ada translated the paper, which had originally been written by an Italian scientist named Luigi Menabrea, she added her own notes. These notes helped make the future computer even more practical. Today, Ada is recognized as one of the first computer programmers!

Although Ada is well known for her accomplishments, she did not live long; she died on November 27, 1852, at the age of 36. She had often been sick throughout her life, and she eventually died due to cancer.

Her work has not been forgotten, though. The British Computer Society awards a medal in her name each year. One of the first computer languages was named

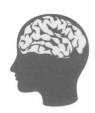

after her and it is simply known as "Ada." Ada Lovelace proved to the world how much women have to offer the world of information technology!

# Words to Know

**Baron:** a member of the nobility.
**Analytical:** relating to the use of logical reasoning.

# Find Out More

Lethbridge, Lucy. *Ada Lovelace: The Computer Wizard of Victorian England.* London: Short, 2004.

San Diego Supercomputer Center, "Ada Byron, Countess of Lovelace"
www.sdsc.edu/ScienceWomen/lovelace.html

Computer History Museum, "Ada Lovelace"
www.computerhistory.org/babbage/adalovelace/

# Algorithms

How do you solve a complex math problem? You use a very specific set of steps. Multiplication should be done before addition, for instance. Steps within parentheses should be solved before exponents. The same sequence is true of computers, except the steps computers follow are even more complex. These sets of steps to complete calculations are known as algorithms. When Ada finished her translation, she included new algorithms in her notes. These algorithms are considered some of the first to be created specifically for use in a computer.

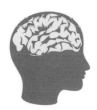

# 3

# Adele Goldstine:
# Programmer of ENIAC, First Digital Computer

Before World War II (1939–1945), most women were not encouraged to work outside their homes. Instead, they were expected to take care of their families. Even fewer women were accepted into scientific fields. When the United States went to war, though, many men were sent overseas to fight for our country. They left behind many jobs that needed to be filled by someone—and now women had a chance to prove what they could do. The war effort also created many more jobs than had existed before, making military equipment and doing research to develop new defense technology. Adele Goldstine was one of the women to take this new opportunity.

Adele was born on December 21, 1920, and grew up in New York City. She was interested in mathematics and went to Hunter College. After graduating with a bachelor's degree, she went next to the University of Michigan, where she earned a master's degree in mathematics. Adele was particularly interested in how mathematics could be applied to the new field of computers. In 1941, she married Herman Goldstine. Like Adele, Herman was interested in mathematics and computers.

Adele worked on a big project that was completed in 1946—a huge computer known as the ENIAC (short for Electronic Numerical Integrator And Computer), which was the first electronic **digital** computer. Unlike the computers of today, the ENIAC needed large cables to bring information from one area of the computer to another. Most of the people who helped to create it were female. It was assembled at the Moore School of Electrical Engineering of the University of Pennsylvania. Adele and several other women did most of the programming for the machine. At the time, programming meant physically moving the cables and dials that made the machine work. When it was completed, Adele wrote the technical description for the machine. The manual she wrote also helped with maintenance, so if the ENIAC ran into functioning problems, people would know how to fix it.

The ENIAC had a very specific purpose, which made it helpful during World War II. The machine used math to help gunners hit their targets. When a bullet is shot, it will eventually be pulled down by gravity. This means that for a bullet to hit a target that is far away, it cannot be shot directly at the target. It must be shot up so that it falls down in an arc. This is similar to how an arrow is shot in archery, except bullets move much faster! The ENIAC was like a giant calculator. It used complex math equations to calculate the angle a bullet needed to be shot at to hit its target. The ENIAC also considered other factors, such as wind, which

# Early Computers

Computers used to be very large. Some of the earliest computers could fill an entire room!

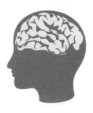

could change the course of a bullet as it flies. Since wind can push a bullet up, down, left, or right, the angle of a gun must be changed accordingly to compensate. The ENIAC allowed these factors to be entered, so that it could give gunners better directions for how to shoot.

Although Adele and her fellow female programmers were very important, they were not treated that way at the time. Women were not originally regarded as scientists, despite how much scientific work they did during World War II. Through their hard work, however, these scientists helped women earn the respect they needed to be accepted as computer scientists.

After World War II, it was still difficult for women to become scientists, but it was easier than it was before the war. Cancer killed Adele Goldstine in 1964, when she was only 43, but she lived long enough to see the ways the world was starting to change, partly because of her work. Women have played large roles in the computer-driven world in which we live today!

# Words to Know

**Digital:** involving computer technology

# Find Out More

Blueproof, "Women's First Roles in the 20th Century Computer World: The ENIAC" www.bluepoof.com/Colloquium/eniac.html

Campbell, Kelly. *Computer: A History of the Information Machine.* Boston: Sloan Technology, 2004.

Raum, Elizabeth. *The History of the Computer.* Mankato, Minn.: Heinemann-Raintree, 2007.

Smithsonian Libraries Unbound, "Women's History Month DIY Project" blog.library.si.edu/tag/adele-goldstine/#.UTayYzBFqSo

Wired, "Women Proto-Programmers Get Their Just Reward" www.wired.com/culture/lifestyle/news/1997/05/3711

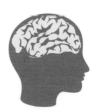

# Erna Schneider: Improving Telephone Communications

**S**ometimes people start out studying one area only to discover that they're interested in another as well. This was what happened with Erna Schneider. She started out studying **philosophy** and history. Through her studies in these subjects, she also learned **logic**, which is a mathematical concept as well. Logic is very important in information technology, and Erna was able to apply her understanding of logic in practical ways. She eventually invented a very important piece of technology. Thanks to her, computerized phone systems are much better than they once were!

Erna was born on June 19, 1926, in New Jersey. She loved spending time outdoors and learning about science. Erna also loved to read about famous women scientists. Their stories told her that a woman could be successful, so she set her own goals high.

When Erna went away to college, however, she did not major in science. She graduated from Wellesley College in 1948 with a bachelor's degree in history and philosophy. She went on to graduate school, where she continued her studies in philosophy. There she became interested in the application of logic to mathematics.

Only three years after earning her bachelor's degree, Erna earned a PhD from Yale University in 1951. She became a professor at Swarthmore College, where she taught philosophy and logic.

Logic has a very important role in programming. All computer programs are based on human logic. This is because machines created by humans interpret computer programs. Erna's understanding of logic helped her begin her studies in information technology.

In 1954, Erna left Swarthmore and joined Bell Labs. At about this time time, the way call centers handled telephone calls was changing. Up until now, human beings had transferred calls from line to line, but now computer programs were starting to handle calls. This also made it easier for large businesses to manage their phone lines. However, there was one problem: sometimes, more calls came in than the

# Inventions in Action

Erna's invention was patented back in 1971. However, you can still see her ideas at work today. Have you ever called the phone number for a large company and gotten an automated message that either puts you on hold or asks you to call back later? Although it may seem frustrating, this allows the business to drop calls when there are more coming in than its system can handle. It keeps the entire system from crashing when lots of people are calling the same number at once.

computer program could handle. This made the call center very unstable. If it got jammed, it could break down. Erna used her knowledge of logic and programming to fix this problem.

First she analyzed how calls were handled. She discovered that during certain times of day, more calls arrived than at other times. Erna needed to find a way to

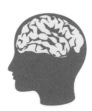

limit the calls being accepted so that the whole program did not crash. She did this by writing a computer program that was so successful it completely changed how call centers worked. Companies now appeared more professional because their phone systems were more reliable.

Erna's invention was named "Feedback Control Monitor for Stored Program Data Processing System." It is her most famous creation, but not her only one. For her hard work, Erna was promoted to a technical supervisor. She was the first female to hold this position. Erna continued to work at Bell Labs until 1987, when she left after thirty-two years of work in the field of computer technology applied to telephones.

Following her retirement, Erna didn't stop working, though. Her next project was to improve education for young women. She had not forgotten how discouraged she felt as a child, and the drive she had needed to have to succeed. Today she helps other women gain recognition in the field.

# Words to Know

**Philosophy:** the study of the nature of knowledge, reality, and existence.
**Logic:** a system of symbols and math used to guide computers to do tasks.

# Find Out More

Brown, David. *Inventing Modern America*. Boston: MIT Press, 2003.

Greenblatt, Jacquelyn A. *Women Scientists and Inventors: A Science Puzzle Book*. Culver City, Calif.: Good Year, 2008.

Massachusetts Institute of Technology,
"Inventor of the Week: Erna Schneider Hoover"
web.mit.edu/invent/iow/hoover.html

Meagan Pollock, "Women in STEM: Erna Schneider Hoover"
meaganpollock.com/women-in-stem-erna-schneider-hoover

Wellesley Alumnae, "Alumnae Achievement: Erna Schneider Hoover '48"
academics.wellesley.edu/Alum/Awards/AAA/winners/hoover.html

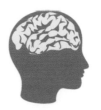

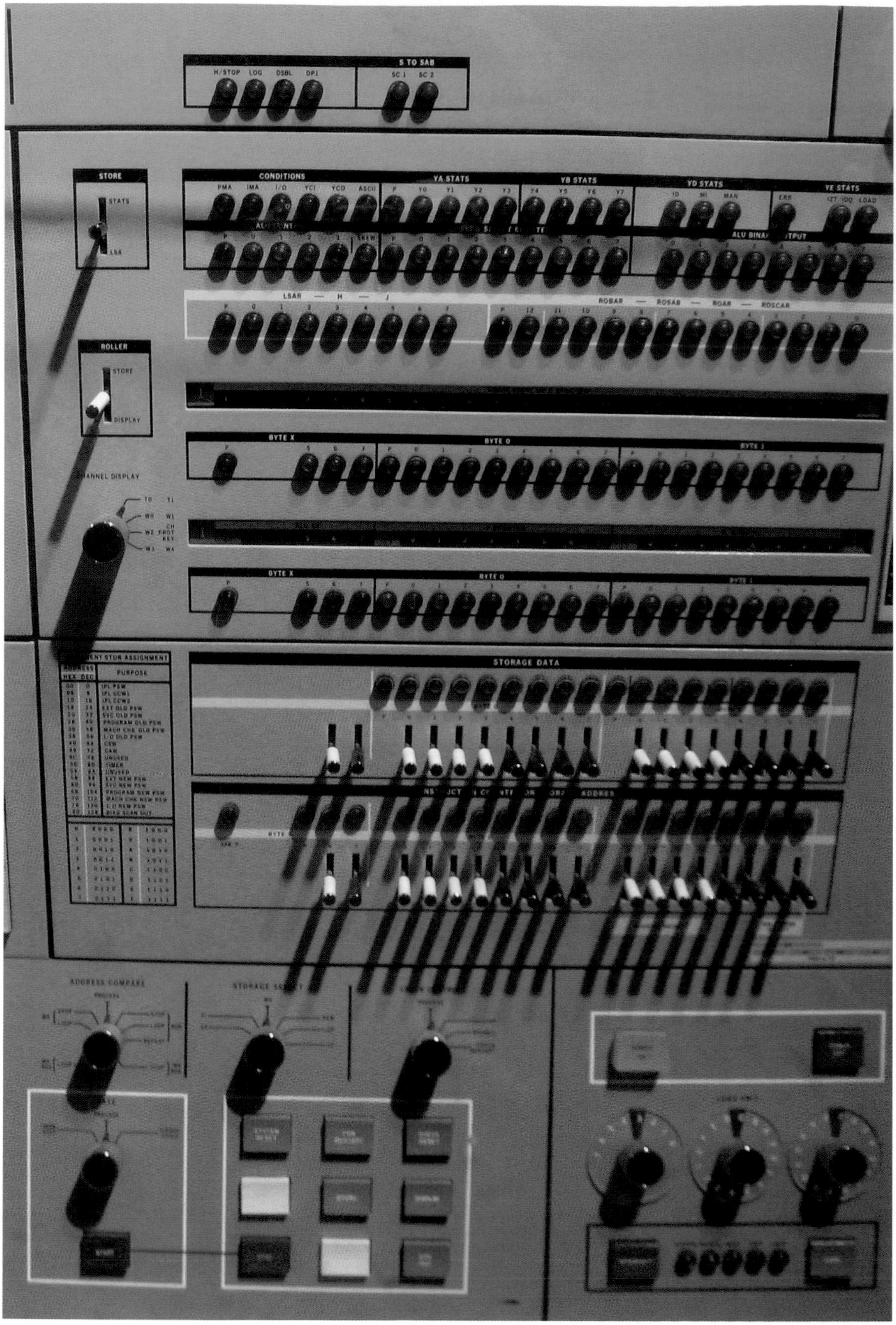
S TO SAB
H/STOP
LOG
DSBL
DP1
SC 1
SC 2
STORE
STATS
LSA
CONDITIONS
PMA
IMA
I/O
YA STATS
YB STATS
YD STATS
YE STATS
LSAR
ROBAR
ROSAB
ROAR
ROSCAR
ROLLER
STORE
DISPLAY
CHANNEL DISPLAY
BYTE X
BYTE 0
BYTE 1
STORAGE DATA

# 5

# Jean E. Sammet:
## Computer Language Developer

J ean E. Sammet became one of the first female experts in a specific area of computer science. As a programmer, she wrote in special languages that were used to tell a computer what to do. Without her hard work, computer programming would not be what it is today.

Jean E. Sammet was born in 1928 in New York City. Her interest in mathematics started at a young age. As a little girl, she took all of the math classes she could. In 1948, she earned a bachelor's degree in mathematics from Mount Holyoke College. Just one year later, Jean earned a master's degree in math from the University of Illinois. She never pursued a PhD, although she did earn an **honorary** one thirty years later.

In 1955, Jean began working at Sperry Gyroscope, a company that built electronics and other equipment. This was her first job in the computer field. As an expert mathematician, she supervised a group of scientific programmers. Three years later, she joined another company known as Sylvania Electric Products.

Jean worked on many projects here including software for an early computer known as MOBIDIC (Mobile Digital Computer) that was used by the United States Army. At the time, computers were very large and this one needed to be loaded onto a trailer so that it could be transported.

At the same time, Jean was working with the CODASYL (Conference on Data Systems Language) Short Range Committee. This group was working to create a common computer language that could be used by businesses, so that each business didn't have to create and use its own. COBOL, which is short for Common Business-Oriented Language, was the result of the committee's work. It is now known as one of the oldest programming languages. Jean had helped make computer history!

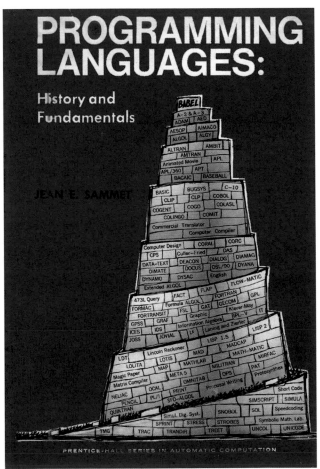

Some scientists choose to share their knowledge with the world beyond the scientific community by writing a book. In Jean's case, she wanted to teach people about the history of computing languages. When she published her first work in 1969, it was praised as an "instant computer classic." Many people used it to understand the history behind computer languages. Others read it and thought about what the future of programming might hold.

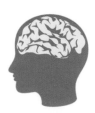

# Grace Hopper: Another Woman Who Helped Lay IT Foundations

Grace Hopper (December 9, 1906–January 1, 1992) is often referred to as the "mother of the COBOL language." She was an American computer scientist and a U.S. Navy Rear Admiral. A pioneer in the field of information technology, she developed the first compiler for a computer programming language. A compiler takes code that people use and converts it into machine code (which most people can't understand, but which the computer can read). Compilers are used today to write the programs we use in our computers every day.

Grace is also credited with coming up with the term "debugging" for fixing computer glitches. According to the story, the term came about when Grace had to remove an actual moth from a computer. Because of the breadth of her accomplishments, she is sometimes referred to as "Amazing Grace."

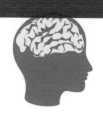

# What Is Symbolic Math?

If you've studied algebra in school, you have used a type of symbolic math. When a number is not known, a symbol—such as n, x, or y—is used to represent the unknown number in a mathematical equation.

Jean's experience helped her become a manager for IBM in 1961 at the Boston Programming Center. While Jean was working at IBM, she helped develop FORMAC. Short for Formula Manipulation Compiler, FORMAC was another computer language, one of the first that was used to complete symbolic mathematical formulas. FORMAC allowed Jean to apply her knowledge to math and computers.

In 1969, Jean wrote an important book titled *Programming Languages: History and Fundamentals*. It became very popular and helped her become even more recognized as an expert in her field. Jean also spent some time teaching graduate courses at Adelphi University.

Later in life, Jean became an even bigger part of the computing world. She joined the Association for Computing Machinery (ACM), and in 1974, she became the first female president of this group. Two years later, she was **inducted** into the National Academy of Engineering. Although she never earned a PhD, Jean was given an honorary one in 1978 from Mount Holyoke College, where she had earned her bachelor's degree. In 1979, Jean helped develop another computer language known as Ada, which was named after Ada Lovelace.

Jean's work as one of the first developers has made her famous. In 1985, she received the ACM Distinguished Service Award. Four years later, she was given the Augusta Ada Lovelace Award from the Association for Women in Computing. Finally, in 2001, she was given one of the highest honors by being named a Computer History Museum Fellow. Jean proved that women have a lot to offer to information technology!

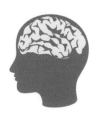

# Words to Know

**Honorary:** something given to a person, such as an award or academic degree, without the person having fulfilled the normal requirements.

**Inducted:** formally admitted into something, such as a club or organization.

# Find Out More

Abbate, Janet. *Recoding Gender: Women's Changing Participation in Computing.* Boston: MIT Press, 2012.

American University in Bulgaria,
"Women in the History of Computing Technology: Jean E. Sammet"
cssu-bg.org/WomenInCS/jean_sammet.php

Computer History Museum, "Jean Sammet"
www.computerhistory.org/fellowawards/hall/bios/Jean,Sammet

IEEE Computer Society, "Jean E. Sammet"
www.computer.org/portal/web/awards/sammet

Williams, Kathleen Broome. *Grace Hopper: Admiral of the Cyber Sea.* Annapolis, Md.: U.S. Naval Institute Press, 2004.

# 6

# Anita Borg:
## Supporting Women in IT

When Anita Borg first became a computer scientist, not many women were doing what she did. The few female scientists who were working in the field did not usually communicate with each other. Anita Borg wanted to change that. What better way than to use the technology that she worked on to do it? Anita started a mailing list using e-mail. She called it Systers, and it helped women in information technology keep in touch with each other. At the time, e-mail was very new; the women who joined Systers were impressed by how convenient it was. Anita had helped unite the skilled women working in IT, so that they could work together more easily.

Anita was born on January 17, 1949. As a child, she spent time in Illinois, Hawaii, and Washington. Growing up, she was interested in mathematics, but it wasn't until she went away to college that she started studying computers. In 1981, Anita earned a PhD in computer science from New York University.

One of Anita's first jobs was to help design operating systems. Operating systems are large software programs that control everything a computer can do. Two of the most well-known operating systems are Windows and Mac. These operating systems act as a framework for the modern computer. Many of the other programs we use—like word processors and Internet browser—would not function without an operating system.

When Anita started working, one of the successful operating systems was known as Unix. She helped develop another system based on this one.

As a female scientist, Anita understood the special challenges women face in the IT industry. In 1987, while attending a technical conference, she realized that only a few computer scientists were female—and she decided to do something about it. She went home and started Systers. This mailing list was only for female scientists within any field that had to do with information technology. Systers' goal was to help women in information technology get ahead, but it was also meant to inspire other young women to get involved.

After starting Systers, Anita Borg took another step to help female scientists. Along with Telle Whitney, she founded a conference known as the Grace Hopper

# Unix and Linux

Today, Unix is not as common as other operating systems, since it is outdated and very limited in what it can do. A more recent version, based off the original Unix design, is known as Linux. Unlike Unix, Linux is frequently updated—and better yet, it's free to use. Some of the most powerful computers now use Linux as their operating system.

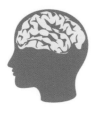

# A More Connected World

As technology advances, people are becoming more connected. It is easy to take this for granted when you grow up with this technology, but there was a time when it was not possible. Even calling another country was expensive and hard to do. Imagine an even earlier world where all communication was done through letters—messages written on paper and carried by horse or boat to other parts of the world. Today, you can video chat in real time with someone on the other side of the world!

Celebration of Women in Computing. This gathering invited women in information technology to share recent discoveries and interests. The first of these conferences was held in 1994, and they are still held today. Three years after the first conference, Anita founded the Institute for Women and Technology. This **nonprofit** organization encourages women to join scientific fields. It also helps female scientists find success in their field. Today, it is known as the Anita Borg Institute for Women and Technology.

In 1995, Anita was awarded the Augusta Ada Lovelace Award. She died on April 6, 2003, but she left behind her mark on the world, and she had received many awards for her work helping women. A scholarship named in her honor, the Google Anita Borg Memorial Scholarship, continues to carry on her **legacy**.

# Words to Know

**Nonprofit:** an organization that uses money made to further a social cause.
**Legacy:** memory and gifts left behind when a person dies.

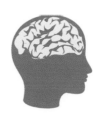

# Another Woman in the IT Field

Telle Whitney received a bachelor's degree in computer science from the University of Utah in 1978 and a PhD in computer science from Caltech in 1985. She moved to Silicon Valley to work in the computer chip industry, creating chips and the software that supports them. She held senior technical management positions at large computer companies, as well as senior roles at several startup technology companies. She is currently CEO and president of the Anita Borg Institute for Women and Technology.

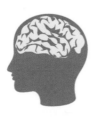

# Find Out More

American University in Bulgaria
"Women in the History of Computing Technology: Anita Borg"
www.cssu-bg.org/WomenInCS/anita_borg.php

Anita Borg Institute
www.anitaborg.org

Google, "The Google Anita Borg Memorial Scholarship"
www.google.com/anitaborg

Ryan, Johnny. *A History of the Internet and the Digital Future.* London, UK: Reaktion Books, 2013.

# 7

# Radia Perlman: Contributor to the Creation of the Internet

Although Radia Perlman is sometimes referred to as the "mother of the Internet," she shakes her head whenever she hears the title. Radia knows she was not the only person to help create the Internet. There were plenty of other important people involved as well. Radia also dislikes the fact that her gender is used in the title—she feels strongly that gender shouldn't have anything to do with the respect she has earned as a scientist.

Radia Perlman was born in Virginia in 1951. She attended Massachusetts Institute of Technology (MIT) for both undergraduate and graduate studies. Her bachelor's and master's degrees were in mathematics, while her PhD was in computer science.

While going to school, she helped create an educational robotics language. Later known as LOGO, this computer language helped children program robots. One of the youngest children to participate was only six years old! Even as a student in college, Radia was already teaching others about computers.

In addition to being a scientist, Radia was also an inventor. Some of her ideas were completely new and **innovative**. She has received dozens of **patents** for her many inventions. One of her most famous is known as Spanning Tree Protocol, which allows multiple computers to communicate with each other over a network. A woman of many talents, Radia has even written a poem about how the Spanning Tree Protocol works:

I think that I shall never see
A graph more lovely than a tree.
A tree whose crucial property
Is loop-free connectivity.

# Networks

For computers, networks are very important. When you use a computer at school, for example, it is often linked to other computers within the school. You can access files and even communicate with other people on the same network. Many businesses rely on these local area networks (LANs), because they are private. Many young adults participate in LAN parties, where they get together to play games together. Gaming conventions use LANs as well, so that attendees can participate in an enormous LAN party.

Before networks existed, this was not possible. Computer scientists like Radia helped make networks efficient and stable. The Internet works in a similar way, but unlike smaller networks, the Internet links billions of people around the world.

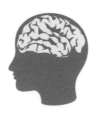

A tree which must be sure to span.
So packets can reach every LAN.
First the Root must be selected
By ID it is elected.
Least cost paths from Root are traced
In the tree these paths are placed.
A mesh is made by folks like me
Then bridges find a spanning tree.

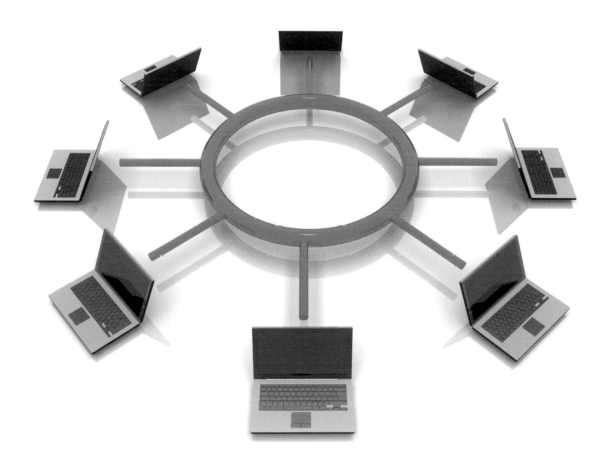

Radia created technology that allowed computers to link with each other.

Radia Perlman 43

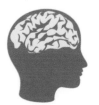

Because of Radia's hard work, networks are now very advanced. Her work on networks eventually led to the advancement of the Internet, while local area networks (LANs) like the ones she worked on are still used today.

As computers **evolve**, so do our uses for them. For example, we need to be able to keep safe the information that's stored on them. How do you prevent a burglar from walking into your house and stealing all of your valuable items? Locking the doors at night would be a good way to start. Your parents might have also installed a security system to let you know if someone breaks in. Just like houses, computers are vulnerable to attack. When networks and the Internet first started to be used, security became a very big concern. Businesses and personal users stored a lot of important things on their computers that they did not want anyone to see. Radia and other scientists like her worked to increase computer security.

Radia has worked at many important companies, including IBM and Sun Microsystems. Her knowledge and experience continue to improve networks today.

Another **passion** of Radia's is educating others. In addition to working for companies, she also taught at several universities, such as Harvard and MIT. She has also written several books about networks and network security.

Radia has received many awards for her work in this field. One of the most important is the Anita Borg Institute Women of Vision Award, which she received in 2005. Radia has also been named as one of the twenty most influential people by *Data Communications* magazine in two separate issues.

She has her reasons for disliking the title "mother of the Internet"—but she's certainly earned the respect she's been given.

# Words to Know

**Innovative:** consisting of new methods or technology; creative and original.
**Patents:** the rights to produce and sell an invention, given by the government.
**Evolve:** to develop, get more complex.
**Passion:** an intense love for something or someone.

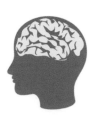

# Find Out More

American University in Bulgaria,
"Women in the History of Computing Technology: Radia Perlman"
www.cssu-bg.org/WomenInCS/radia_perlman.php

Baker, David. *Internet Safety for Kids*. New York: Self-Esteem Zone, 2013.

IT World, "Why IEEE Fellow Radia Perlman Hates Technology"
www.itworld.com/networking/158579/advice-engineers-ieee-fellow-radia-perlman

Network World, "Q&A: Sun's Radia Perlman Speaks Out on Being Stuck with IP, New Life for Spanning Tree and Her Answer to Data Security: The Ephemerizer"
www.networkworld.com/news/2006/050506-sun-radia-perlman-interview.html

Silicon Valley Watcher, "Intel's Radia Perlman"
www.siliconvalleywatcher.com/mt/archives/2011/04/profile_of_radi.php

# 8

# Eva Tardos:
# Exploring Algorithms

**S**ome computer scientists do research, some create inventions, and others teach. In Eva Tardos' case, she has done all three. She is currently a professor at Cornell University, and she is also the editor-in-chief of the SIAM Journal on Computing.

Eva Tardos was born in Hungary in 1957. She went to college in Budapest, Hungary, at Eötvös University. She graduated with a PhD in mathematics in 1981. Not long after, she went to the United States, where she became a visiting professor at the Massachusetts Institute of Technology (MIT). After two years, she began working at Cornell University.

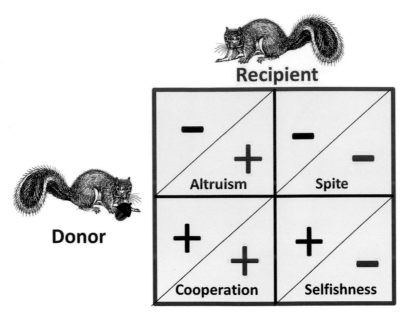

**Recipient**

**Donor**

|  |  |
|---|---|
| **−** **+** Altruism | **−** **−** Spite |
| **+** **+** Cooperation | **+** **−** Selfishness |

This image diagrams game theory as applied to the interactions between two squirrels. Each squirrel has two options: reacting to the exchange of an acorn either positively or negatively. As a result, there are four possible outcomes to the squirrels' interactions.

Like many mathematicians, Eva had a **specialty**. She liked algorithms, the sets of steps that tell a computer how to solve a problem. Algorithms can be found in almost every area of computer science, but Eva was most interested in graphs and networks. Algorithms must be first created and then tested by computer scientists; Eva helped design new algorithms as well as analyze the algorithms that were already created. By testing algorithms, IT scientists discover any problems they might have. Then they must come up with ways to fix them, before they can actually be used in computers.

Another area Eva researched combined game theory and algorithms. Game theory is something that is often studied in **economics**. It examines how people interact and make decisions. Algorithmic game theory uses algorithms to do the same thing. In the future, it could help companies understand better ways of **marketing**.

In 1989, Eva Tardos joined Cornell University as a professor. In addition to teaching, she is a member of many organizations. As the editor-in-chief of the *SIAM Journal on Computing*, Eva helps educate the computer scientists of tomorrow. Another publication she is a part of is the *Journal of the Association for*

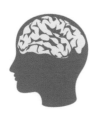

*Computing Machinery* (ACM). Eva is part of the editorial board for this journal as well. She has also co-authored two books and written many papers.

Eva Tardos has received many awards in her lifetime. She was given the Fulkerson Prize in 1988 for her work in mathematical programming. Her other awards include the NSF Presidential Young Investigator Award and several teaching awards from Cornell University. More recently, she was the department chair of computer science at Cornell. Eva has also received many **fellowships**. With these fellowships, Eva could continue learning and helping others.

Today, Eva continues to teach at Cornell University. As a successful female scientist, Eva is a role model for every student she teaches in her classes, especially the young women. She uses her experience as a female scientist to inspire and guide young women who may one day follow in her footsteps.

# Words to Know

**Specialty:** an area of expertise.
**Economics:** the study of how people produce, distribute, and consume resources.
**Marketing:** the way a business promotes and sells products and services.
**Fellowships:** money given to students for specific research purposes.

# Find Out More

American University in Bulgaria, "Women in the History of Computing Technology: Eva Tardos"
cssu-bg.org/WomenInCS/eva_tardos.php

Cornell University, "Eva Tardos"
www.cs.cornell.edu/people/eva/eva.html

Harbour, Jonathan S. *Video Game Programming for Kids*. Boston: Course Technology PTR, 2012.

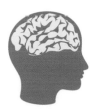

# 9

# Shafi Goldwasser:
## Cryptographer

It's hard to imagine the world without the Internet. The Internet has connected the world and allowed people access to nearly limitless information. However, the Internet also has dangers and problems. Sometimes, for example, people try to steal important information over the Internet. IT scientists like Shafi Goldwasser work hard to prevent this by using a special field of computer science known as cryptography.

Shafrira Goldwasser was born in New York City in 1958. She attended Carnegie Mellon University, where she earned a bachelor's degree in mathematics in 1979. From there, Shafi went to the University of California at Berkeley to focus on computer science. She eventually earned both a master's degree and a PhD in the field.

She got a job at the Massachusetts Institute of Technology (MIT). There, she not only taught but also did research, especially in cryptography.

Have you ever used a cipher—a secret code—to send a message to a friend? If you did, you were using cryptography. People have been encrypting messages—using secret codes—to keep their communications secret for more than three thousand years. Cryptography was once used primarily during wartime, to pass messages without the risk of the enemy getting hold of important information. In today's computer age, encryption is even more important, though it's much more sophisticated than it once was.

The secret codes you may have used just for fun are not complicated enough to be used in the real world. It's too easy to crack their code! Spies use cryptography—but so do banks and businesses. Every time you use a computer password, you're using a form of encryption.

Many times, scientists make discoveries that open up whole new worlds of possibility. One discovery leads to another. Shafi Goldwasser started out working on interactive and zero-knowledge proofs. These turned out to have practical **security** applications.

A zero-knowledge proof is the way a computer can give an answer to a question without giving any more information than necessary. For instance, when you buy an item online using a credit card, the website needs to check to see if the credit card number is correct. It would be dangerous if any of your credit card information was stored on the Internet, though. Instead, the website only determines if it is correct or incorrect and returns that information. That way, no one can steal your credit information because it remains secure.

Shafi Goldwasser has been recognized with several awards and has won the Gödel Prize two times in her life. In 1996, she also received the Grace Murray Hopper Award, which is given to the "outstanding young computer professional of the year." In 1997, Shafi became the first person to receive an RSA

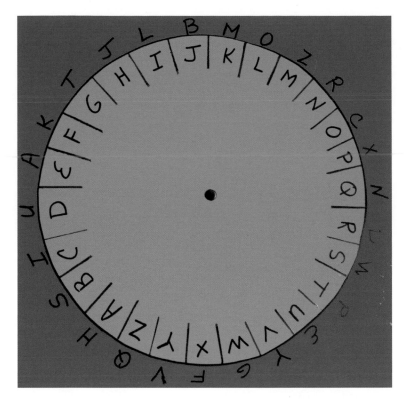

This is a simple cipher you can make to create your own secret code. Each time you turn the wheel, the letters will line up differently, creading a new code.

Professorship at MIT, and she was given the RSA Award in Mathematics for her work in cryptography in 1998. More recently, she received the Athena Lecturer Award and the Benjamin Franklin Medal in Computer and Cognitive Science.

Shafi continues to teach at MIT today as a professor of electrical engineering and computer science. At the same time, she is also a professor of computer science and applied mathematics at the Weizmann Institute of Science in Israel. She follows in the footsteps of women like Ada Lovelace and Adele Goldstine, who helped lay the foundations for information technology—and Shafi is blazing a trail that other women can follow as well.

# Words to Know

**Security:** protection from danger.

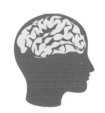

The Enigma machine used during World War II was an early form of the technology Shafi uses today.

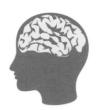

# Computers and Spies

During World War II, the Germans used Enigma, a cipher machine, to develop nearly unbreakable codes for sending messages. Enigma's settings offered 150,000,000,000,000,000,000 possible solutions—and yet the Allies were eventually able to crack its code. By end of the war, the Allies were reading 10 percent of all German Enigma communications on the world's first electromagnetic computers.

Enigma was just the beginning of how complex cryptography has become. In today's world—where people store and send secret data digitally—ciphers have become increasingly complex. Today, all of this is done automatically without you even knowing it. Shafi Goldwasser is one of the people we have to thank for this.

# Find Out More

American University in Bulgaria, "Women in the History of Computing Technology: Shafi Goldwasser"
cssu-bg.org/WomenInCS/shafi_goldwasser.php

Beissinger, Janet. *The Cryptoclub: Using Mathematics to Make and Break Secret Codes.* Wellesley: A.K. Peters/CRC Press, 2006.

Massachusetts Institute of Technology, "Shafi Goldwasser"
people.csail.mit.edu/shafi

Singh, Simon. *The Code Book: The Science of Secrecy from Ancient Egypt to Quantum Cryptography.* New York: Anchor, 2000.

# 10

# Opportunities for Women in Information Technology

Information technology is a growing field. Although there are still far more men in this field than there are women, many universities are trying to encourage women to pursue computer science. Some of them offer scholarships to young women who want to enter this field.

Once you have your degree in this field, the job opportunities will vary, depending on the level of your education and the particular IT field you wish to enter.

# IT Research Scientists

Computer and information research scientists invent and design new technology and find new uses for existing technology. They study and solve complex problems in computing for business, science, medicine, and other uses.

Employment of computer and information research scientists is expected to grow by 19 percent from 2010 to 2020, about as fast as the average of all occupations. Computer and information research scientists are likely to enjoy excellent job **prospects**, as many companies have a hard time finding a sufficient number of these highly skilled workers. This is the highest-paid job within the IT field.

# Computer Programmers

Computer programmers write code to create software programs. They turn the program designs created by software developers and engineers into instructions that a computer can follow.

Employment of computer programmers is expected to increase 12 percent from 2010 to 2020, about as fast as the average for all occupations. Since computer programming can be done from anywhere in the world, companies often hire programmers in countries that have lower wages, which means that it may be harder for American programmers to find jobs.

# Computer Support Specialists

Computer support specialists provide help and advice to people and organizations using computer software or equipment. Some, called technical support specialists, support IT employees within their organization. Others, called help-desk technicians, assist non-IT users who are having computer problems.

Employment of computer support specialists is expected to grow 18 percent from 2010 to 2020, about as fast as the average for all occupations. Job prospects should be favorable. Applicants with a bachelor's degree and a strong technical background should have the best job opportunities.

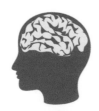

Job opportunities for women in IT have come a long way since this picture was taken. The women here are entering data onto punched cards that were used by IBM computers in the 1950s.

# Computer Systems Analysts

Computer systems analysts study an organization's current computer systems and procedures and make recommendations to management to help the organization operate more efficiently and effectively. They bring business and information technology together by understanding the needs and limitations of both.

Employment of computer systems analysts is expected to grow 22 percent from 2010 to 2020, faster than the average of all occupations. A greater **reliance** on computer systems in many kinds of businesses and organizations will lead to an increased demand for this occupation.

# Database Administrators

Database administrators use software to store and organize data, such as financial information and customer shipping records. They make sure that data are available to users and are secure from **unauthorized** access.

Employment of database administrators is projected to grow 31 percent from 2010 to 2020, much faster than the average for all occupations. Rapid growth in data collection by businesses, as well as increased need for database security measures, will contribute to the growth of this occupation.

# Information Security Analysts, Web Developers, and Computer Network Architects

These positions all use information technology (IT) to advance their organization's goals. Security analysts ensure a firm's information stays safe from **cyberattacks**. Web developers create websites to help firms have a public face. Computer network architects create the internal networks all workers within organizations use.

Employment of information security analysts, web developers, and computer network architects is projected to grow 22 percent from 2010 to 2020, faster than the average for all occupations. Job prospects for all three occupations should be favorable.

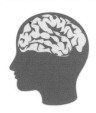

Today, all around the world (even in Afghanistan!) girls have opportunities to learn about computers.

# Software Developers

Software developers are the creative minds behind computer programs. Some develop the applications that allow people to do specific tasks on a computer or other device. Others develop the underlying systems that run the devices or control networks.

Employment of software developers is projected to grow 30 percent from 2010 to 2020, much faster than the average for all occupations. The main reason for the rapid growth is a large increase in the demand for computer software.

# A Growing Field

The world today depends on computers. Businesses of all sorts rely on information technology. So do schools and churches. And so do families and individuals.

If computers fascinate you, this could be a good career to consider. Other women have broken the trail for you—now you can follow in their footsteps! Who knows? You might find new paths all your own.

# Words to Know

**Prospects:** possibilities or likelihoods.
**Reliance:** dependence on or trust in.
**Unauthorized:** not having permission.
**Cyberattacks:** efforts to destroy or cause damage to computer systems.

# Find Out More

Bureau of Labor Statistics, "Occupational Outlook Handbook:
Computer and Information Technology"
www.bls.gov/ooh/computer-and-information-technology/home.htm

Reeves, Diane Lindsey, and Gail Karlitz. *Career Ideas for Teens in Information Technology*. New York: Ferguson's, 2012.

Rutgers, "Career Opportunities for Majors in Information Technology and Informatics"
careerservices.rutgers.edu/informatics.shtml

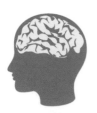

# Index

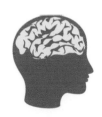

# About the Author & Consultant

Shaina Indovino is a writer and illustrator living in Nesconset, New York. She graduated from Binghamton University, where she received degrees in sociology and English. She enjoyed the opportunity to apply both her areas of study to a topic that excites her: women in science. She hopes more young women will follow their calling toward what they truly love, whether it be science related or not.

Ann Lee-Karlon, PhD, is the President of the Association for Women in Science (AWIS) in 2014–2016. AWIS is a national non-profit organization dedicated to advancing women in science, technology, engineering, and mathematics. Dr. Lee-Karlon also serves as Senior Vice President at Genentech, a major biotechnology company focused on discovering and developing medicines for serious diseases such as cancer. Dr. Lee-Karlon holds a BS in Bioengineering from the University of California at Berkeley, an MBA from Stanford University, and a PhD in Bioengineering from the University of California at San Diego, where she was a National Science Foundation Graduate Research Fellow. She completed a postdoctoral fellowship at the University College London as an NSF International Research Fellow. Dr. Lee-Karlon holds several U.S. and international patents in vascular and tissue engineering.

# Picture Credits

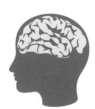